D1179099

# Purple Ronnie's
## Little Book for a
# Smashing
# DAD

## by Purple Ronnie

First published 2006 by Boxtree
an imprint of Pan Macmillan Ltd
Pan Macmillan, 20 New Wharf Road, London N1 9RR
Basingstoke and Oxford
Associated companies throughout the world
www.panmacmillan.com

ISBN 978-0-7522-2565-4

9 8 7 6 5 4

A CIP catalogue record for this book is
available from the British Library.

Text by Giles Andreae
Illustrations by Janet Cronin
Printed by Proost, Belgium

...mmm

cool beer

Dad Time

who's kids are these?
much too early
jump
groan
hee hee
frrp
bounce
wriggle
scamper

## Remember

All dads deserve a lie in
just once in a while

## Rules of Being a Dad - Nº1

You must always have a go at fixing things even if you've got no idea what you're doing

complete rubbish
the flange socket has definitely come out of the gasket trembler
oh no!
TOOLS
gush

# ☆ Special Tip

Sometimes the smallest room in the house is a dad's best hiding place

The great thing about being a dad is that you get to be in charge of the remote control

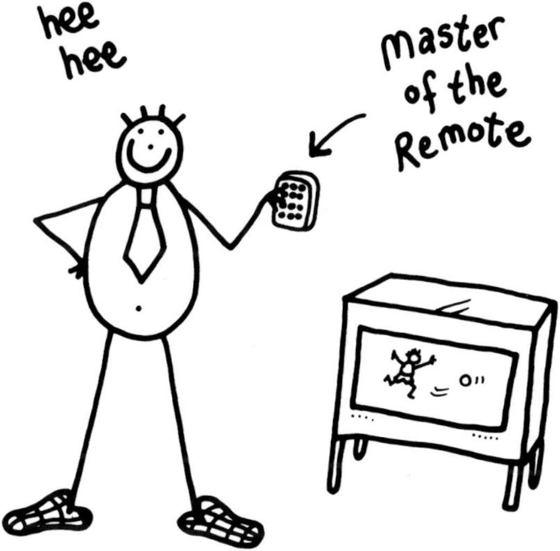
hee
hee
Master
of the
Remote

## Rules of Being a Dad - Nº 2

Your wallet is really just a cash machine for your children

## Interesting Fact

Dads' tummies almost always get bigger after they have had children

It's so I can see what you must have gone through, my darling
hrumph
great big belly

## Dads and the Newspaper

When dads read the newspaper, it is hardly ever the news that they are really looking at

# Rules of Being a Dad - N°3

Never attempt to be trendy.
Old pants with holes in
are usually best

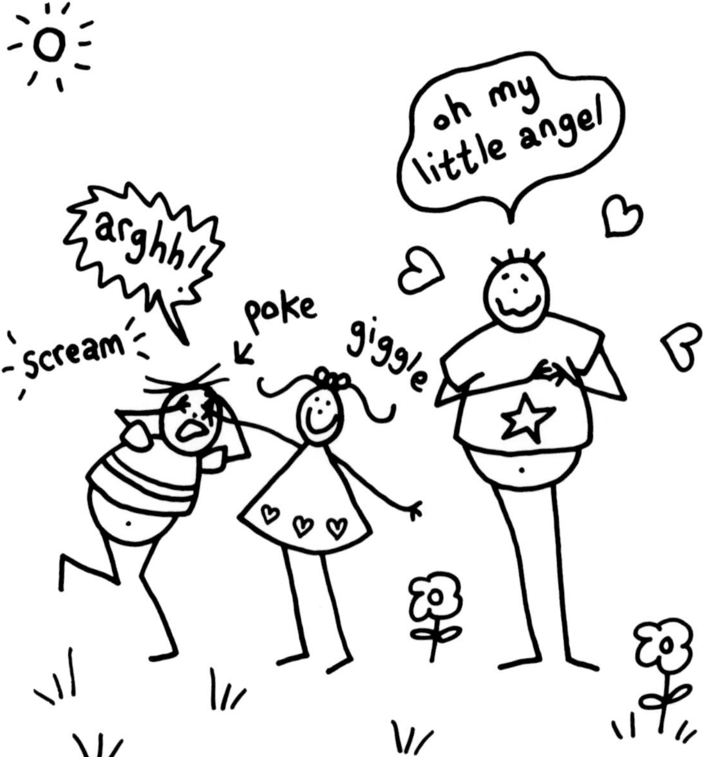
oh my little angel
arghh!
scream
poke
giggle

## Dads and their Daughters

Sometimes it can be hard for daddy's little girl to do anything wrong at all

☆ **Special Tip**

Just once in a while
it is nice to let your
dad win at football

## Rules of Being a Dad - Nº 4

If it's your house, you can fart wherever you like

Sometimes, all a dad needs at the end of the day is a nice big drink

# Dads and the Telephone

To most dads - the telephone is the enemy

## Rules of Being a Dad - N°5

Your car is a taxi and you are the unpaid driver

# Growing Up

Some Mums can't bear the idea of their little darlings growing up.
Most dads can't wait

## Warning

Some dads just aren't made for DIY

## Rules of Being a Dad - Nº 6

Dads don't get letters.
Dads just get bills

Some dads are never happier than when they're pottering in the garden

Compost

RECYCLE STUFF

SEEDS

brrr

lovely
lawn

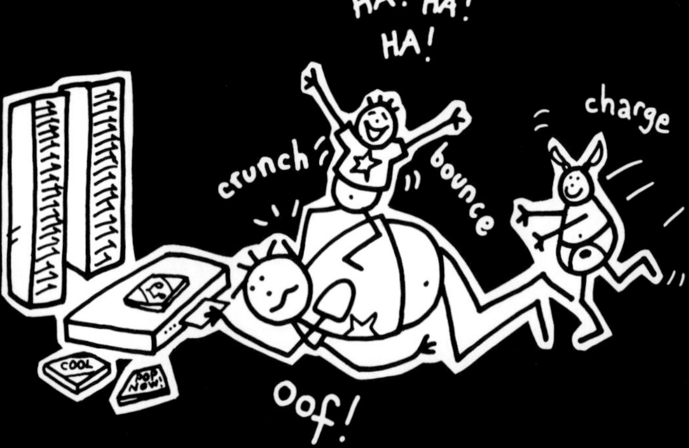
HA! HA!
HA!
crunch
bounce
charge
COOL
POP NOW!
oof!

# Warning

To little children, a dad is sometimes just a great big climbing frame

## Rules of Being a Dad - N°7

When you've got your slippers on, the world becomes a better place

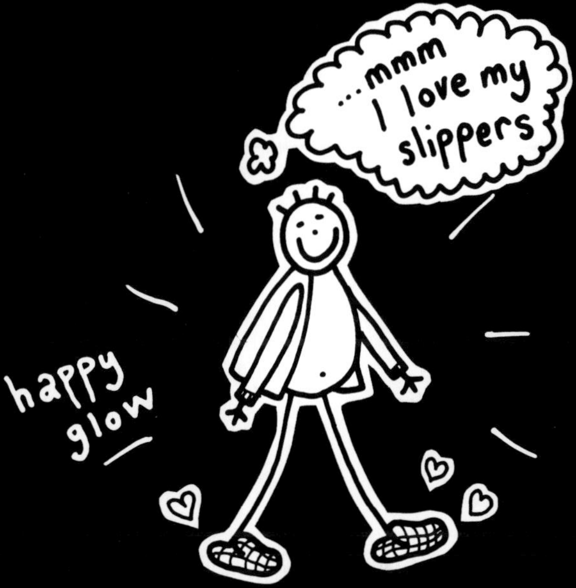
...mmm I love my slippers
happy glow

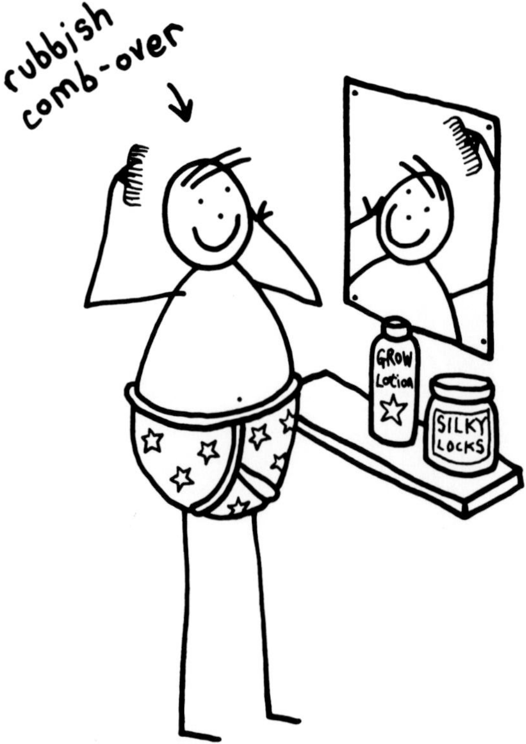
rubbish comb-over
GROW Lotion
SILKY LOCKS

Some dads will do anything to make it look like they've still got loads of hair

☆ **Special Tip**

There are some jobs that only a dad can do

rubbish singing
i'm a boogie woogie machine
a bit tipsy
no rhythm
v. bad trousers
isn't that your dad?
no

## Rules of Being a Dad - N°8

Never _ever_ dance in front of your children

Dads can be very useful in all sorts of difficult situations

um, can I have my son's ball back please...
scary boys
gulp
v. brave
shake
DIE

NON-DAD

DAD

## Dads' Fantasies

When you become a dad,
your favourite fantasies
start to change

## Rules of Being a Dad - Nº9

You are completely in charge of directions wherever you go

## ☆ Special Tip

Mums have special ways of getting dads to do things for them

## Warning

No one else even thinks about sitting in dad's favourite armchair

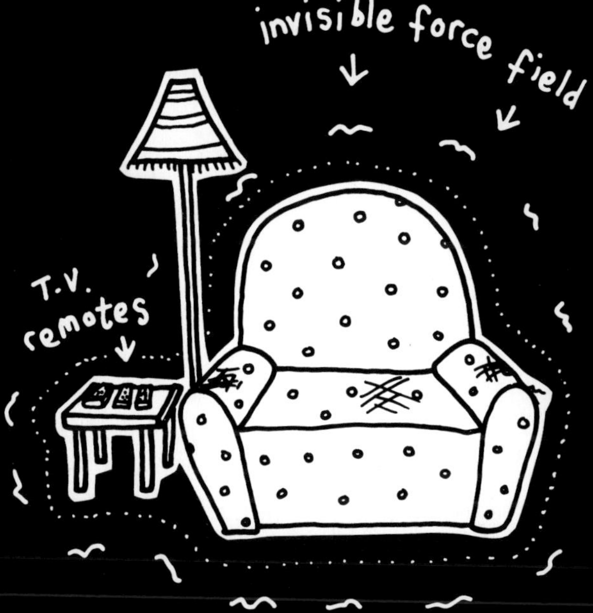
invisible force field
T.V. remotes

## Rules of Being a Dad - Nº 10

However much stuff there is to carry, you are the only one who has to carry it

## ☆ Special Tip

Sometimes, all a dad needs to be happy is a little bit of peace and quiet